ChordTime® Piano

Rock 'n Roll

2010 EDITION

Level 2B

I-IV-V⁷ chords in keys of C, G and F

I-IV-V^7 chords in keys of C, G and F

This book belongs to: _____

T0057139

Arranged by

Nancy and Randall Faber

Production Coordinator: Jon Ophoff
Design and Illustration: Terpstra Design, San Francisco
Engraving: Dovetree Productions, Inc.

FABER

PIANO ADVENTURES®

3042 Creek Drive
Ann Arbor, Michigan 48108

A NOTE TO TEACHERS

ChordTime® Piano Rock 'n Roll is a fun-filled collection of rock and roll favorites arranged for the Level 2B pianist. The style and rhythmic appeal of the songs makes this the perfect motivational book for many students.

Not only entertaining, this book is also educational. Written with the teacher in mind, the book provides instruction on basic chord patterns. The keys are limited to C, G, and F. Warm-up exercises orient the student to the I, IV, and V^7 chords and the selections feature two of the most common rock-and-roll progressions—the 12-bar blues and the I-vi-IV-V pattern. Hearing these patterns in the music, the student is able to learn the fundamentals of harmony in a most enjoyable manner.

ChordTime® Piano Rock 'n Roll is part of the *ChordTime® Piano* series. "ChordTime" designates Level 2B of the *PreTime®* to *BigTime® Piano Supplementary Library* arranged by Faber and Faber.

Following are the levels of the supplementary library which lead from *PreTime®* to *BigTime®*.

PreTime® Piano	(Primer Level)
PlayTime® Piano	(Level 1)
ShowTime® Piano	(Level 2A)
ChordTime® Piano	(Level 2B)
FunTime® Piano	(Level 3A-3B)
BigTime® Piano	(Level 4-above)

Each level offers books in a variety of styles, making it possible for the teacher to offer stimulating material for every student. For a complimentary detailed listing, e-mail faber@pianoadventures.com or write us at the mailing address below.

Visit **www.PianoAdventures.com**.

Helpful Hints:

1. The chord warm-ups for a given key should be practiced daily before playing the songs.

2. The student can be asked to identify the I, IV, and V^7 (and vi) chords in each song, and to write the correct chord symbol below the bass staff.

3. When a chord progression is presented in a warm-up, it can be found in subsequent songs. The student can be guided to recognize the pattern where it occurs.

4. Hands-alone practice is recommended to ensure correct fingering and accurate rhythm.

ISBN 978-1-61677-021-1

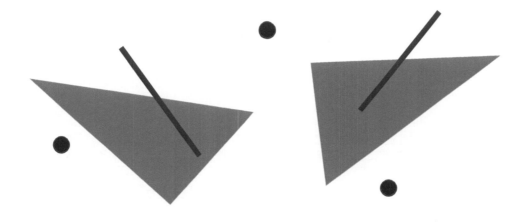

TABLE OF CONTENTS

I, IV, V⁷ Chords in Key of C

Surfin' Safari 4

Crazy Little Thing Called Love..........................6

Yesterday..8

Witch Doctor *(Alvin and the Chipmunks)* 10

Lost in the Fifties Tonight.................................12

I, IV, V⁷ Chords in Key of G

Long Tall Texan 14

Wipe Out 16

Rock Around the Clock 18

You Really Got Me...20

I, IV, V⁷ Chords in Key of F

Mr. Tambourine Man......................................22

Chantilly Lace...24

In the Midnight Hour.....................................26

Come Sail Away...28

Music Dictionary 29

Key of C

Practice these warm-ups before playing the songs in the key of C.

Warm-up 1

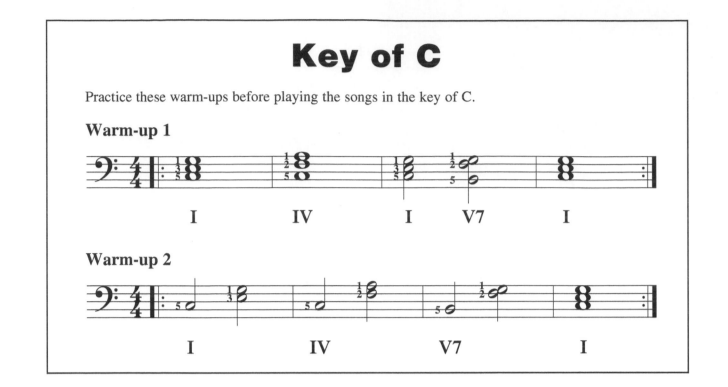

Warm-up 2

Surfin' Safari

Words and Music by
BRIAN WILSON and MIKE LOVE

Bright Rock beat

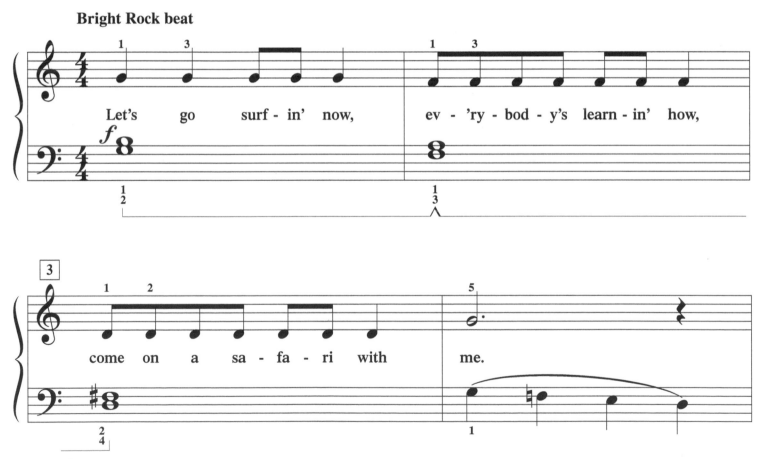

Let's go surf-in' now, ev-'ry-bod-y's learn-in' how,

come on a sa-fa-ri with me.

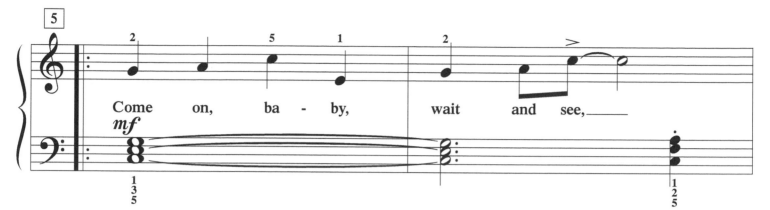

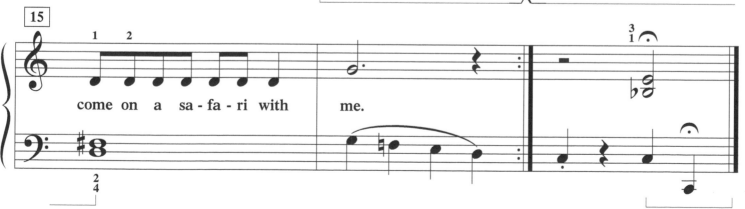

FF1021

Crazy Little Thing Called Love

Words and Music by
FREDDIE MERCURY

Moderate rock beat

thing   called   love.   it   cries *(like a baby)* in (a)

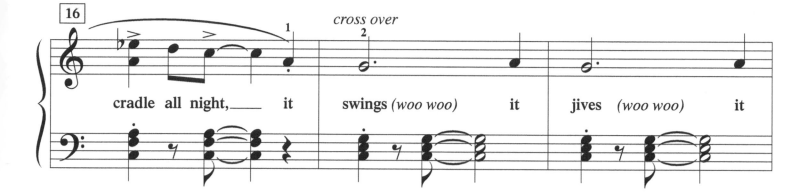

cross over

cradle all night,____ it   swings *(woo woo)* it   jives *(woo woo)* it

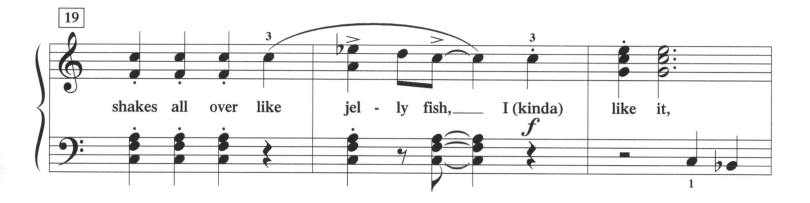

shakes all over like   jel - ly fish,____ I (kinda)   like it,

f

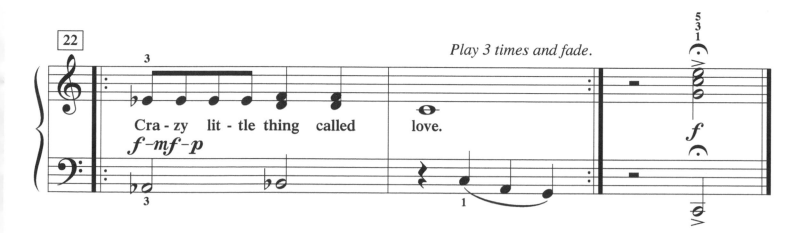

Play 3 times and fade.

Cra - zy lit - tle thing called   love.

f-mf-p

f

Yesterday

Words and Music by
JOHN LENNON and PAUL McCARTNEY

9

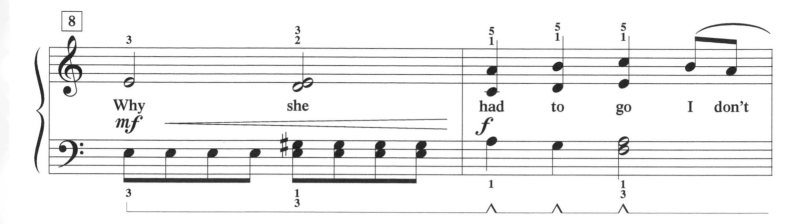

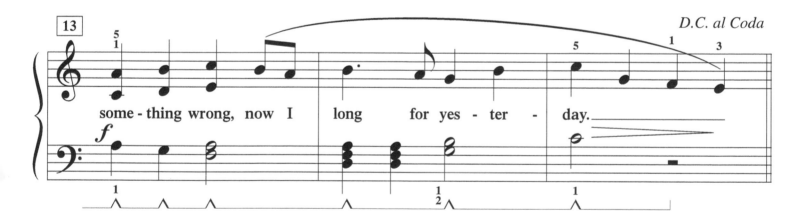

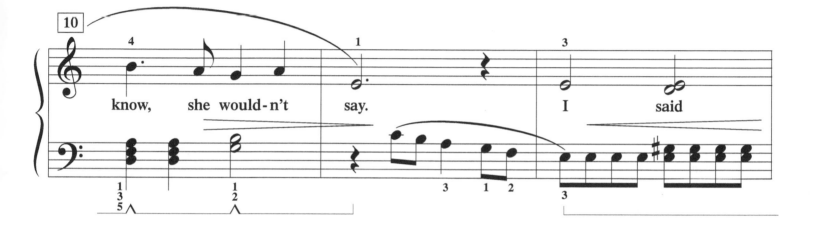

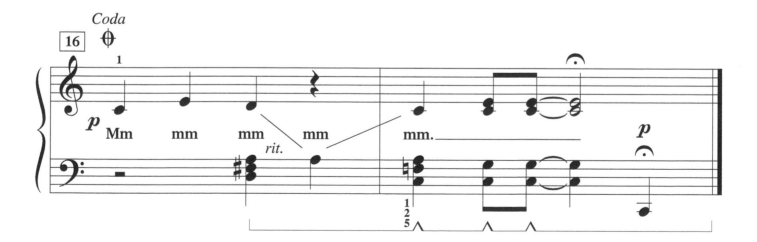

FF1021

Witch Doctor

(Alvin and the Chipmunks)

Words and Music by
ROSS BAGDASARIAN

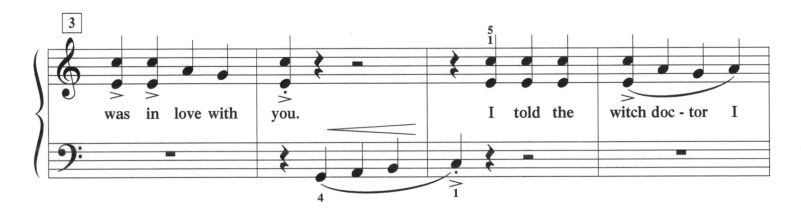

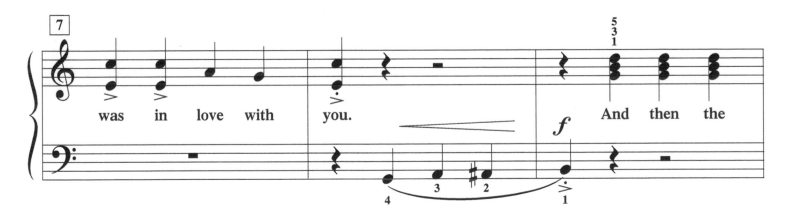

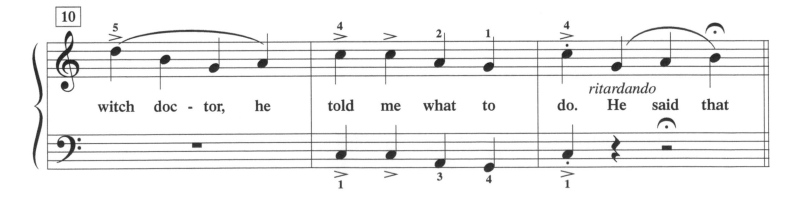

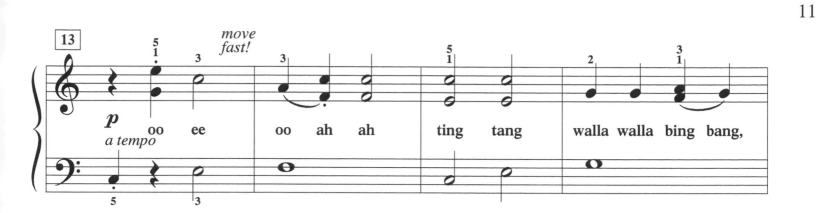

FF1021

Lost in the Fifties Tonight

(In the Still of the Night)

Words and Music by
MIKE REID, TROY SEALS
and FRED PARRIS

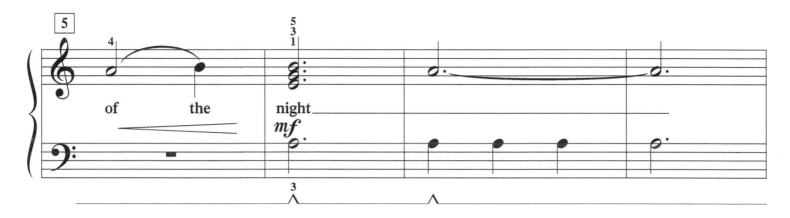

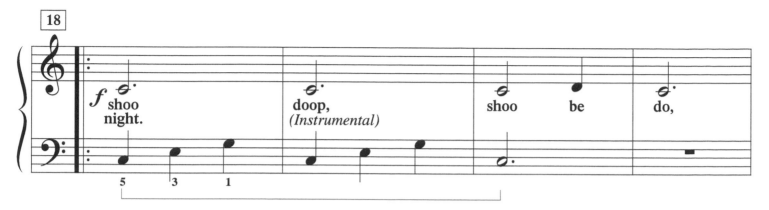

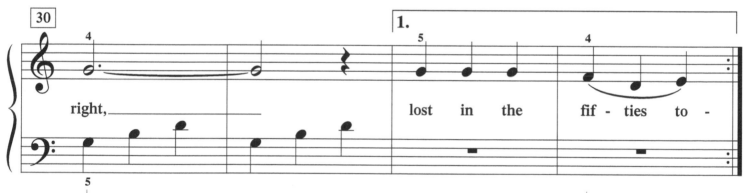

Key of G

Practice these warm-ups before playing the songs in the key of G.

Warm-up 1

Warm-up 2

Long Tall Texan

By HENRY STRZELECKI

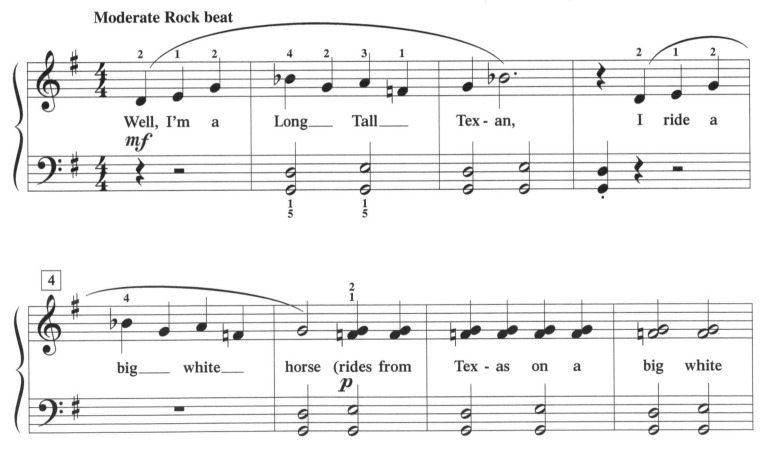

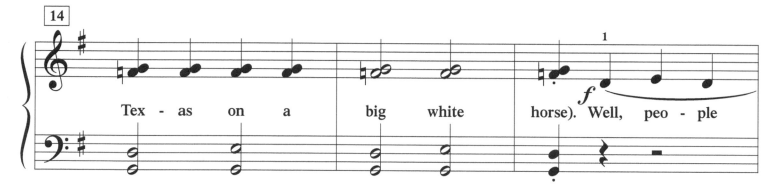

Wipe Out

By SURFARIS

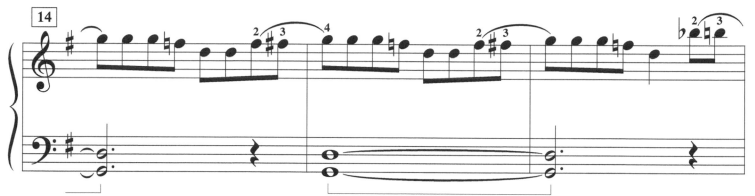

Rock Around the Clock

Words and Music by
MAX C. FREEDMAN and JIMMY DeKNIGHT

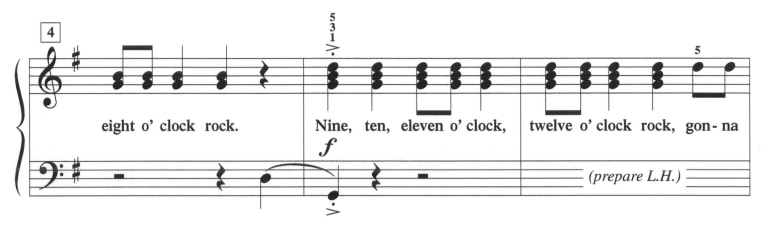

One, two, three o' clock, four o' clock rock. Five, six, seven o' clock, eight o' clock rock. Nine, ten, eleven o' clock, twelve o' clock rock, gon-na

rock a-round the clock to-night.___ Put glad rags on and clock strikes two and

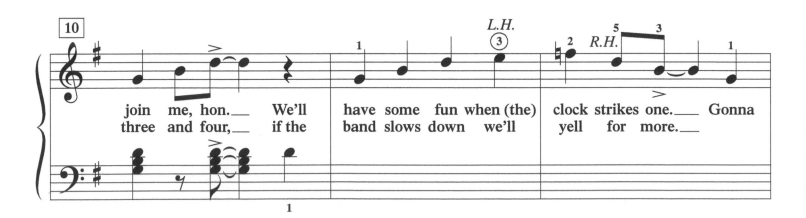

join me, hon.___ We'll have some fun when (the) clock strikes one.___ Gonna
three and four,___ if the band slows down we'll yell for more.___

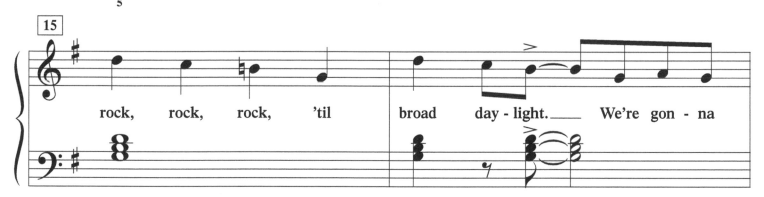

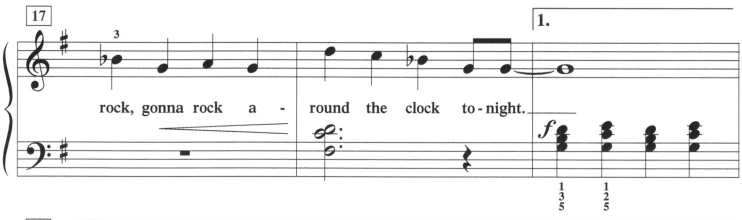

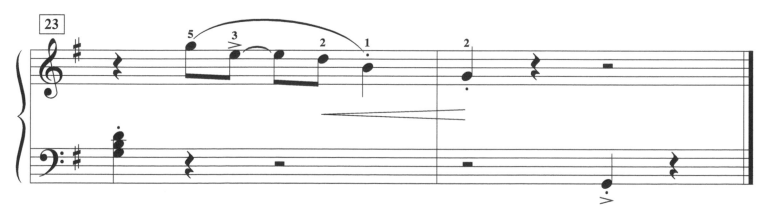

You Really Got Me

Words and Music by
RAY DAVIES

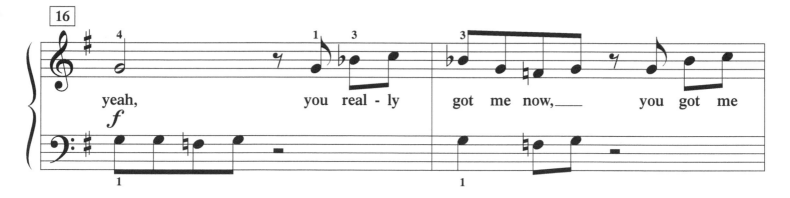

Key of F

Practice these warm-ups before playing the songs in the key of F.

Warm-up 1

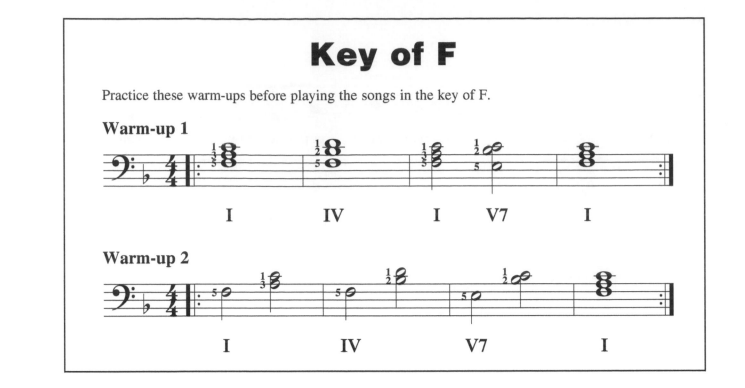

I   IV   I   V7   I

Warm-up 2

I   IV   V7   I

Mr. Tambourine Man

Words and Music by
BOB DYLAN

Moderately

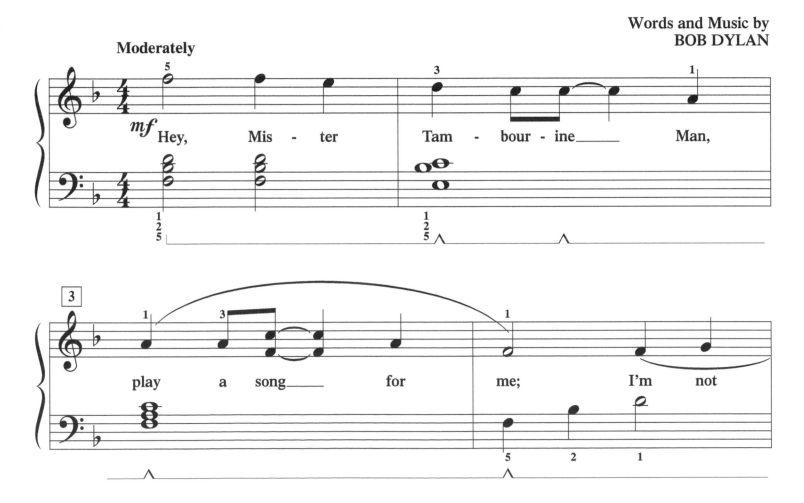

Hey,   Mis - ter   Tam - bour - ine___   Man,

play   a   song___   for   me;   I'm   not

Chantilly Lace

Words and Music by
J.P. RICHARDSON

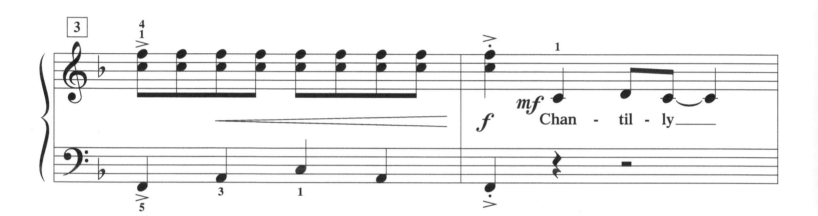

Play the 8th notes in a long-short pattern.

makes the world go 'round. _____ Ain't noth-in' in this world like a

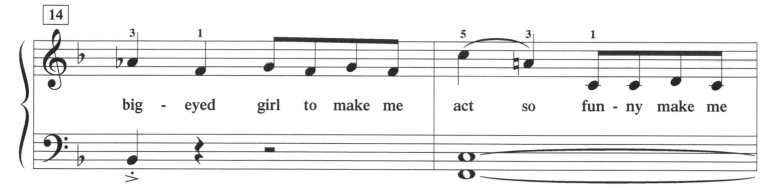

big - eyed girl to make me act so fun-ny make me

spend my mon - ey, make me feel real loose like a

long-necked goose, like a girl.

girl._____

In the Midnight Hour

Words and Music by
STEVE CROPPER and WILSON PICKETT

With a strong Rock beat

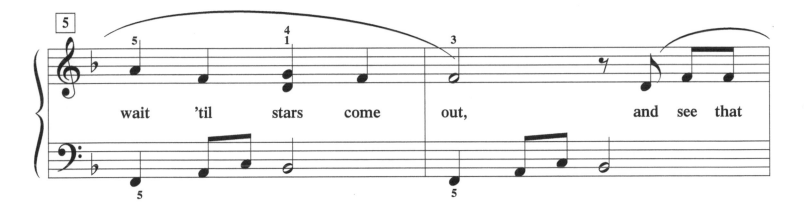

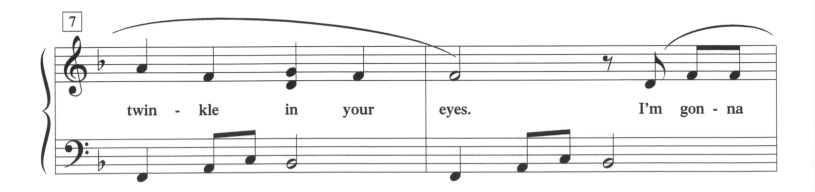

wait 'til the mid-night hour, that's when my love be - gins to

shine. You'll be the on - ly girl I love; I

mp *mf*

real - ly love you so in the mid - night hour.

f R.H. 1 3

dim. *mp*

8va

Come Sail Away

Words and Music by
NANCY FABER